This book is dedicated to my beautiful mother, Sheilah.

MEZZANINE

Table of Contents

Mezzanine *page 6*	**is Beauty** *page 22*
Dear Life, *page 8*	**From dust -** *page 24*
of Revolution *page 10*	**Drawings from a Father** *page 26*
Faith *page 12*	**Bright** *page 28*
Young Joy *page 14*	**Destined** *page 30*
Midnight Again *page 16*	**Beautiful Thing** *page 32*
A Morning *page 18*	**Love in watercolor** *page 34*
Found *page 20*	**into the Ether** *page 36*

MEZZANINE

Table of Contents

Dolls
page 38

Not unlike Birds
page 40

Eyes Closed
page 42

The Peak
page 44

Trying Not To Stare
page 46

The pledge
page 48

Only Love
page 50

Lol, Smile Emoji
page 52

Violent side of love
page 54

Rivers
page 56

Purplehearted
page 58

The Twist
page 60

Trees
page 62

uneasy
page 64

Flags & Banners
page 66

Waiting For Heroes
page 68

Looking down to life
watching - people - passing
thru a sunlit place
The living art,
The textures of humanity
hanging on
gallery white walls
Looking down
to Life
to the assembly
of lives
rolling into lives,
rolling into lives
Unmoved -
Un-motivated to
animate the dolls
People - passing - watching
as destiny disarms
the unwitnessed whys -
In ceaseless procession
so we go -
Until the day is gone

What small Is -
To begin, I guess
I'd say maybe
the many
blades of grass,
which stand
so unconcerned,
contently rooted
in a field
of perfect daises
Lesser more
would be
the humble grains
of sand
that mold
an unforgotten shore,
drinking madly,
from a spilling cup
of oceans

But smallest still,
would be the seconds
of these days,
passing me
like total strangers,
the Tic
Tic,
Tic
- and Tic
of Times,
of Lives entwined
Like words - to a Story
Like birds - to the Sky
No smaller thing is there
Than this,
dear life
of Mine

Does it begin
with uttered words
Which spill like blood
From gaping holes,   Or printed Wounds,
                                       Written with ink
                                          of ill intent

What starts the race inside
Our human minds?   I say,
                                         Find me the womb
                                      Which grows the seeds
                                          Of sweet upheaval
                                                The words
                                             of Revolution

This battered scene reveals
A landscape marred
With craters,
Stained from
Deep extremes   Concocted fears
                                        bomb down upon
                                       The green grasses
                                       Of our imagination
                                           While vigilant
                                       Infantries of Doubt

Forever,
Defend the fears
And always
An impatient peril
To the vitality
Of will -   In this broken land
                              Hope sustains a dying infant,
                                                Her name
                                               Is Change.

At the end
of stringed balloons
Floating into the bright
and blue horizons
of tomorrow,
and today
Leading us over
naive borders
of dreams
with no limits
Summoned by
the songs of storm,
dearest confidant
to a lonely moon
Unafraid and
guarded safely -
in the darkness
and the stars

Such power,
Lies in youthfulness,
To chart a path,
Thru waters unexplored
Does take a special thing,
A Tic - Toc
A beat,
A pulse
Derived from
Faith and feel
To pace the journey
Like gusts of wind
The force of Fates
Does send us out -
To distant lands
Some predetermined,
Some we determine
Across a sea of time
The sum of passing days
Creates a shadow
For our lives -
But youth -
The start,
And spark
Remains always -
A virtue to be prized.

Midnight
the clock, proclaims
in Time
my scripted life
is a Triptych...sigh!
This is
the Good garden itself,
of Evil times -
to the edges
of Why,
travels my cynical mind
As the bough breaks
It's midnight again -
And the cradle falls
And the birds sing

This Day Began,
Like love - songs often do
Beckoning - softly,
What
I meant to it
Wholesome &and Devoted
Day hailed my open eyes
Hazily -
as I arise
From what was -
Arms outstretched,
Reaching for
The pulse of this Today
Thin rays of sun
tickle my subconscious
winding through
A darkened room,
Outside my window
The Song birds dance
With flapping wings -
Here is where
The beauty lies,
In this -
Sublimely grand performance,
Called the morning.

I used to think
of "Love"
as just another
Nothing word -

                        Living my days
                        in honor of myself
                        feasting on pride
                        leaving nothing,
                        but a lofty pile
                        of dirty dishes

    Commitment was
    a corny Joke,
    Meanwhile
    my callous heart
    Fed floods,
    from concrete rivers

                        What strange fruit
                        it seemed,
                        To hurt -
                        To bleed, for Fairytales
                        for Castles

And then -
truth Fell to me

                        Streaking down
                        like comets,
                        trailed by fire
                        and smoke -
                        truth Fell to me

        Struck by
        the lightning
        of attraction,
        and enlightenment

                        Pulled
                        from
                        the flames,
                        into glorious,
                        awaiting Arms

            When you
            affixed onto my soul -
            like magnets touching metal

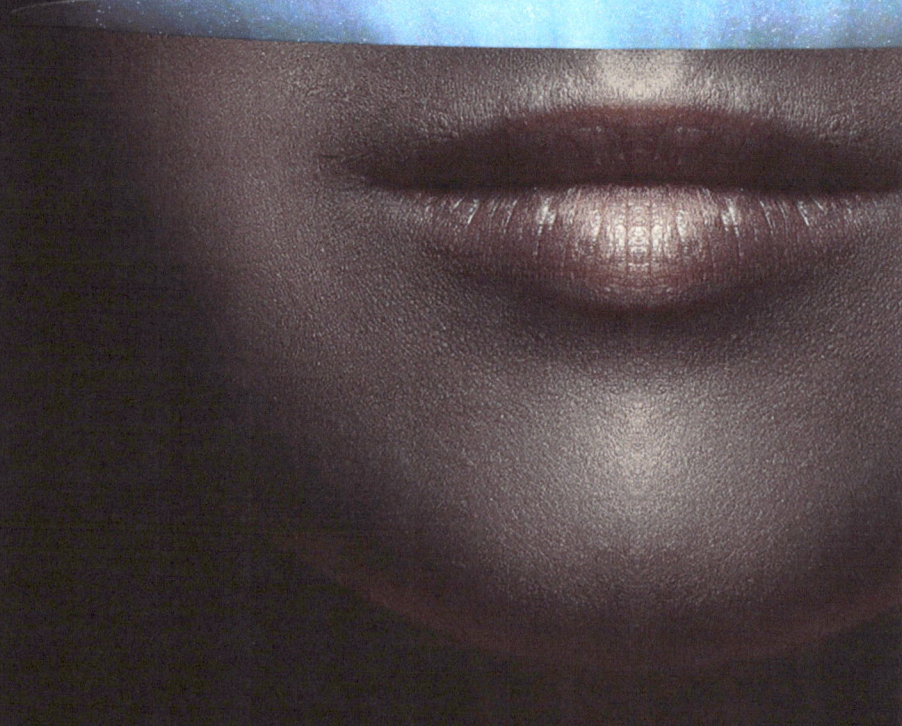

A word which
belies all that you are,
untouched by
what is penned, or spoken
Beyond space and time
a magnetic force
existing like waves,
And stars, and sunsets
The deepest Good
within your eyes
beyond translation
Falling radiantly
into the space
of consciousness,
like the moonlight,
and the sun
A force raging into
this animate world
inhabiting spirit
and body
simply Captivating,
beyond all
Sensory laws -
defying justification
is Beauty -

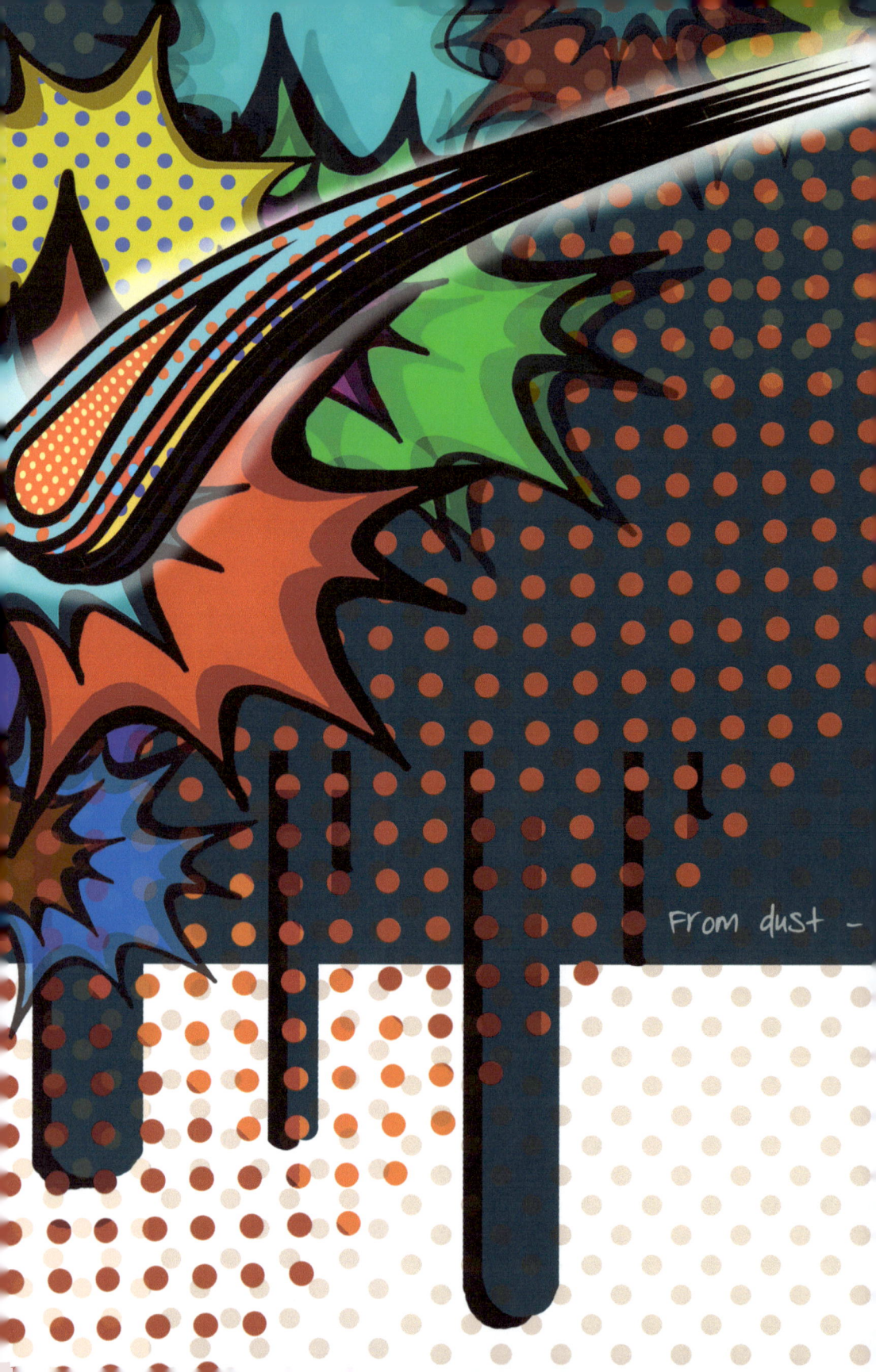

From dust -
Dreams of mine
catch flame
And billow out
like smoke
into the lungs
Of this man-kind
Oppressed ideas
unchained
make jest,
And mock
the fear
that men endure
Inspiration is,
the rescuer -
And the rescued -
emotion is articulated,
innocence is freed
a streaking comet -
Of divine influence collides
Nature with notion -
tangible
materialized -
thru dreams,
From dust

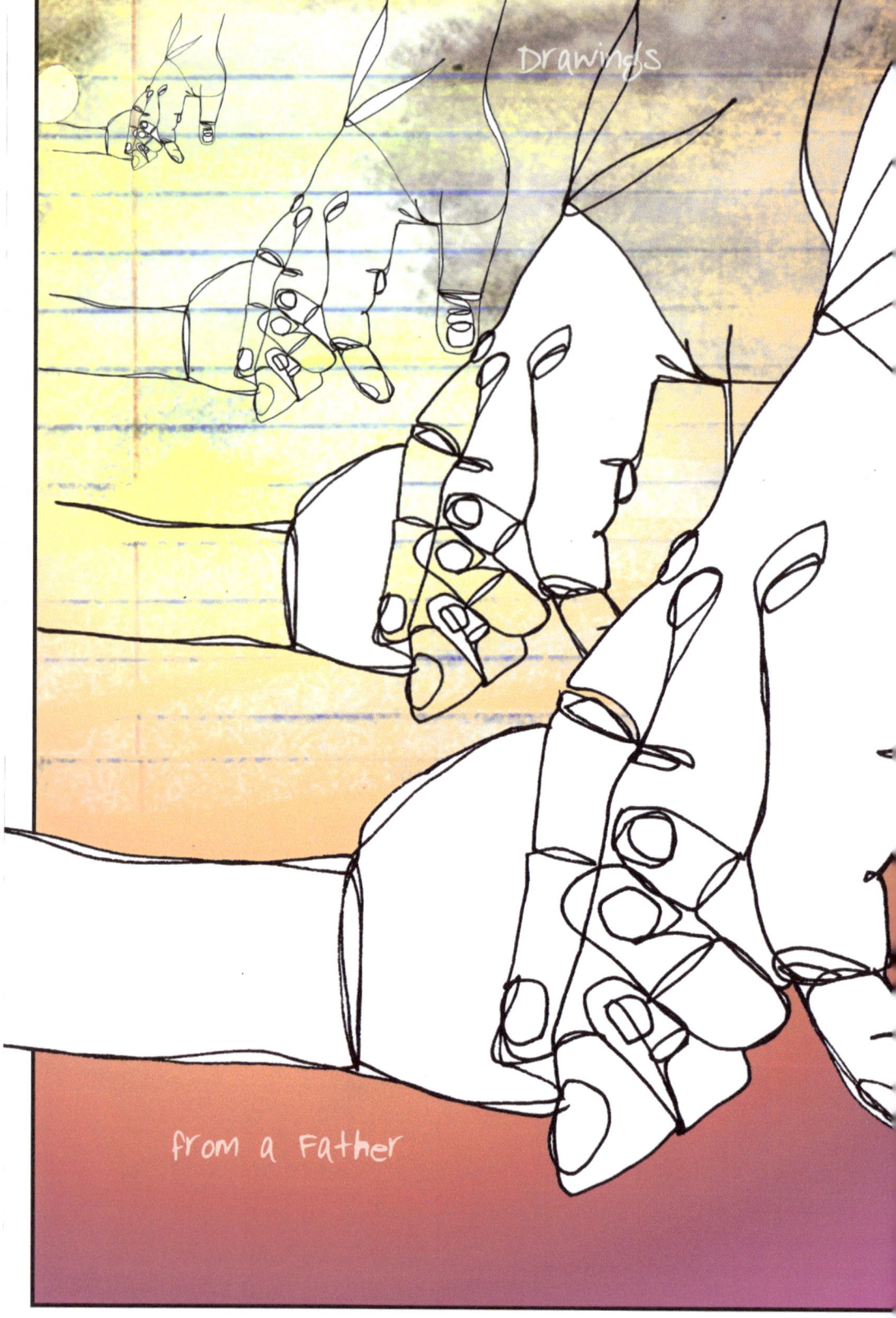

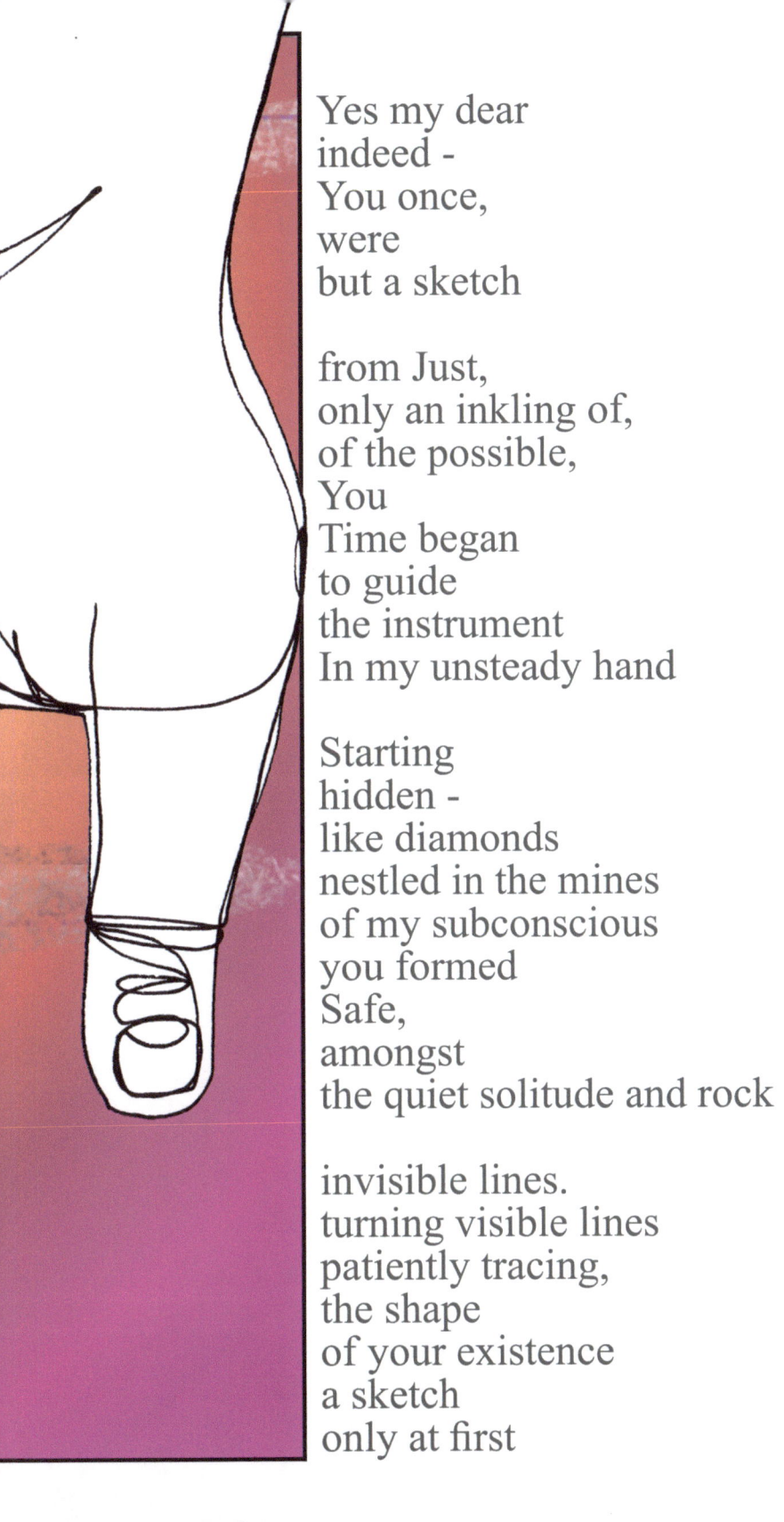

Yes my dear
indeed -
You once,
were
but a sketch

from Just,
only an inkling of,
of the possible,
You
Time began
to guide
the instrument
In my unsteady hand

Starting
hidden -
like diamonds
nestled in the mines
of my subconscious
you formed
Safe,
amongst
the quiet solitude and rock -

invisible lines.
turning visible lines
patiently tracing,
the shape
of your existence
a sketch
only at first

Bright

Today the gifted clouds,
hatch Sun
over the launch point
of my consciousness
and then my body soars
into dream like,
halogen sky -
above the atmosphere
of everything,
and more
on This day
the bluest birds sing
with the urgency of
suffocating fish,
time slipping -
their final gasps
a serenade

Echoes of a song
jog me around corners,
Through a maze of unnamed streets

Then past the watching hills
and winding paths,
Which gossip
my name
To darkened
cobbled roads

From the outskirts of,
No place at all
To where?
To mine -
destiny

I Wonder
what the silent Rose thinks,
so elegant in Bloom
with Mona Lisa eyes
smiling through her perfect
petals

Twas a
Beautiful Thing indeed,
Even though she
couldn't speak to me

In
water color,
dreams,
   of you
emerged on me,
from under
   the edges of
my imagination
A cool and moist
amalgam of luminosity
smeared,
     and brushed
onto the pages
        of my thought
In water color dreams,
   of you -
my heart's poured
liquefied
within the pigment
of your skin -
A delectable conception
of our
immaculate affection -
In my -
water color dreams,
of you

Looking at the sky
She'd wander,
closely to the sun
Undaunted
by the glint and gleam of things
her thoughts would
often spin to dreams
She dreamed
the brightest dreams
With colonies of ants
playing in grass,
And pretty birds
dotting the humble blue
like moving-constellations
Her reveries
Were made of magic
Sublime-sweetest-sustaining,
musical Even -
To which, She moved
To which, I moved
And now
I stare at empty clouds
Blind-sided by the void,
with only emptiness
upon my skin

Into the Ether

And still,
I do have one Reflection
Revealing all
revealing nothing -
boundless
as the Cosmos
In all her essence
my fears resign,
thru a noiseless sphere
of space and time
That, is when
I go adrift into the Ether
of her memory

Prizes of fortune
bely the intentions
of porcelain and glass,
Pretty things

Manufactured
inanimate - toys
to behold,
to Hold

And us,
we All
debauched
and chasing dolls

A moment,
That reminds me of
a storm - Departed

A hurricane of Feeling
like flocks of
doves,
that swoop
and wheel across
the startled sky -
approaching quietly,
But all - at - once
like, accidental mist

No different from
the happy flock of larks,
dressed in smiles
Beneath their beaks -
delighted simply
by a scattering
of seeds

A perfect
weightlessness -
of Earth in orbit,
and
of Us - on it
Soaring

Not unlike
the highest flight
of Eagles

Pity the wanderers
pushed by winds,
unafraid
as sheep
Of a watching world -
Pity the wanderers
blind and numbed
Heading nowhere
from nothing,
dancing for the Moon
like Fireflies -
Broken keys
of a piano
sing the
fractured tune
of tortured souls
As the amputated hands
of Time
bleed seconds -
minutes, and days

So innocent
Delightful
like the deer
My Dear,

Your Presence is
A Sunday
To my Heart,
Which ends
the weak -

Over many
Under none

All that
i've dreamed,
And More

The pinnacle
my Peak.

Trying not to stare
But my,
her Eyes are stairs
Every glance invites
My leaping mind to climb
As I'm preoccupied,
Entwined
by her alluring Air
Trying, trying
Trying!
Not to Stare

Rain down upon my pulse
  squeeze out,
the clouds above
Press your palms
  to mine,
breathe day into my lungs
Lock me tight
  in your embrace
condemn my fears to rot
Banish the heartbreak
  in my hands,
to yesterday- forgotten
Let's mark this hour now
  the last,
Of what's been missed
And, spring up
  like joyous birds
starting our journey with a kiss

It's magic in your eyes,
that takes me,
ever near to bliss
A genie bottle in your smile,
which always,
grants my every wish
And words do not
begin to write,
the story of your heart
As butterflies
exemplify,
the origins of Love

Now.. if you can
just please
not laugh out loud,
My reveal, simply put
is that there's
something -
Completely mysterious
in the light from your eyes -
which has divided me

It takes
my unconscious mind
to someplace -
Live and free
an, All-at-once feeling
What I imagine
flying could feel like;
or drowning would feel like

As doors are unfurled
at the entrance
of your Aura

The walls cower,
and fall
to the feet
of your design

So... please, please, please
don't laugh at me
my darling dear -
PS,
Lol, smile Emoji

Deeper down,
beneath the surface
of pain
and pleasure,
lies a village of hearts
Buried in jagged rock
Unseen,
submerged by Oceans,
A district
of emotion
blossoms from the depths
Deeper down,
sealed in by time
until a yearning
rumbles up
to shake
to crack
the brittle earth

Beautifully destructive -
violent
side of love

Rivers of mine,
Transport me thru
The deepest canyons
I watch my dreams
Shape rock,
And carve out
Magic
From far and distant lands
of my imagination
Wading in the clouds
My toes touch mountains -
And, the sky stares up at me
Then,
not unlike
A lingering glance
Between
Strangers passing
I become
momentarily enchanted,
By the twinkling of stars

Don't dare you wave
goodbye to me
I'm not prepared to Go
First, walk me
down the River Path
and kiss me in the cold
Let's fight to freeze
the moment here
till ice forms on our skin
As all the colour
leaves us
pale and purple in the wind

A precarious
weight
falls upon the Lambs,

Fathered from
storm and cloud -
thrown about
Unkind and treacherous sea

On them,
we place a fractured times

Merciless habits
of the World
handicap
their unformed dreams

Deep in a forest
of branchless trees
from where - will Spring leaves grow

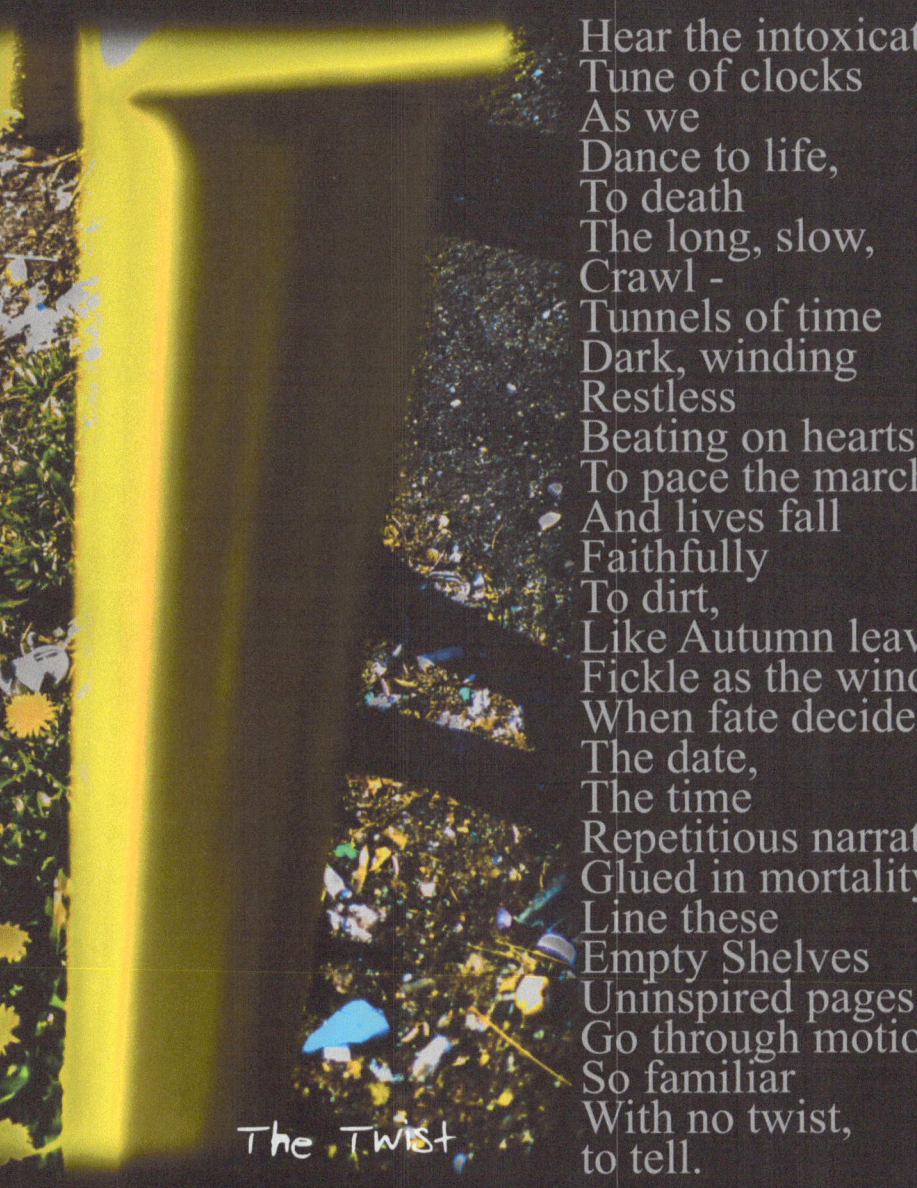

The Twist

Hear the intoxicating
Tune of clocks
As we
Dance to life,
To death
The long, slow,
Crawl -
Tunnels of time
Dark, winding
Restless
Beating on hearts
To pace the march
And lives fall
Faithfully
To dirt,
Like Autumn leaves
Fickle as the winds
When fate decides
The date,
The time
Repetitious narratives,
Glued in mortality
Line these
Empty Shelves
Uninspired pages
Go through motions
So familiar
With no twist,
to tell.

Running streams
glance up at me
beneath
A tangled marsh
The sky above is
swallowed Whole
A feast
to flies and fog
Herrings headed
Home for winter
Flying north this time
As noble stories
Skip their morals
Missing from the psalms
Screaming an
imperfect song
In signature and tune
The Creatures
call to arms begins
Stirring in the dunes
Mired in the nuance
Of a brooding,
bluesy riff
Hope and gloom
Do frolic nude
In my uneasiness

Beneath dark
and solemn remains
are bones of
an impeached defeat

Cascaded upon
like bombs, dropping heavy
on our intellect,
truth becomes a syrupy Surprise

Sown from the seeds
of disingenuous intent,
a prevalent deception
torpedoes Down

Coaxed by dark,
and capricious skies
inscrutable Reigns
beget more rains

As flags and &banners
flank a raging queue
of Caskets

Unified, in protest
to the
Wicked - laws,
which fuel
our hate-filled
wars

Steadfastly
we wait for heroes
Our bravest
Our best, appearing
just in time
to save our delicate,
our fainting lives
Not until steeled
by the depths
of a featured Anguish,
revived by floods
of plight and fear,
and motored by a fuel
to perform Feats
Does one grow able
to defeat the
lonely weariness
of awaiting heroes

Large Print edition
Copyright © 2017 Jean-Pierre Bobo

All rights reserved.

Stephanie Joshi
Akulu Lipenga
───────────
Illustrations

Jean-Pierre Bobo
───────────
Photo Art

www.ingramcontent.com/pod-product-compliance
Lightning Source LLC
Chambersburg PA
CBHW041806160426
43191CB00004B/67